HAL•LEONARD

UKULELE
PLAY-ALONG

AUDIO
ACCESS
INCLUDED

PLAYBACK+
Speed • Pitch • Balance • Loop

VOL. 39

Gypsy Jazz

Play 8 of Your Favorite Songs with Professional Audio Tracks

D0613699

To access audio visit:
www.halleonard.com/mylibrary

Enter Code
4899-7574-4055-8654

Arranged, recorded and performed by Guy Fiorentini

ISBN 978-1-4950-2503-7

HAL•LEONARD®
CORPORATION

7777 W. BLUEMOUND RD. P.O. BOX 13819 MILWAUKEE, WI 53213

Visit Hal Leonard Online at
www.halleonard.com

Coquette

Words by Gus Kahn
Music by Carmen Lambardo and John Green

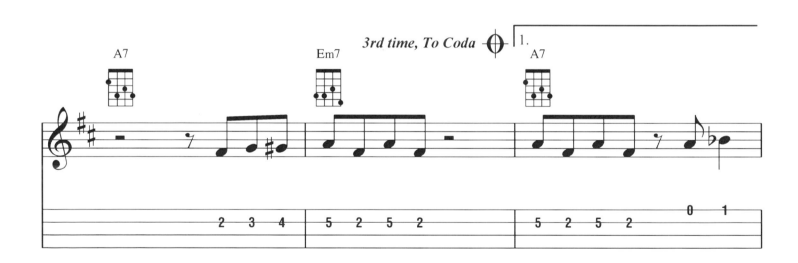

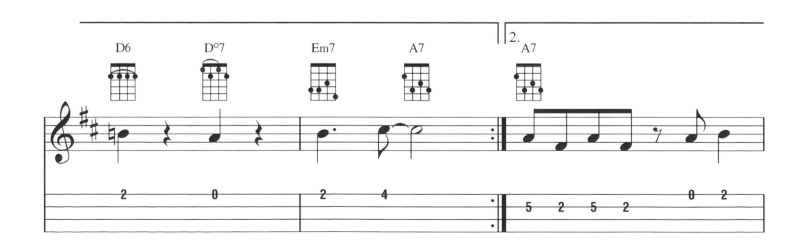

On Play Along track, form is played 4 times.

Dark Eyes

Russian Cabaret Song

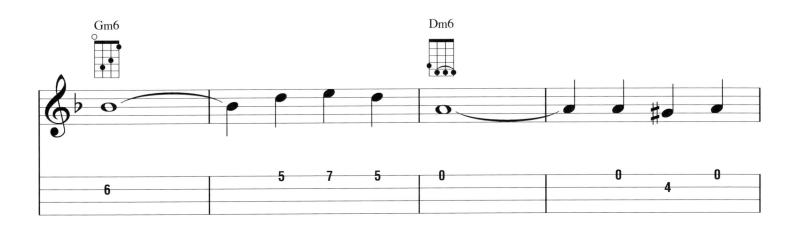

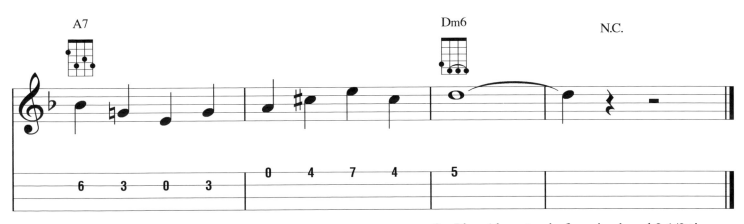

On Play Along track, form is played 2 1/2 times.

Douce Ambiance

By Django Reinhardt

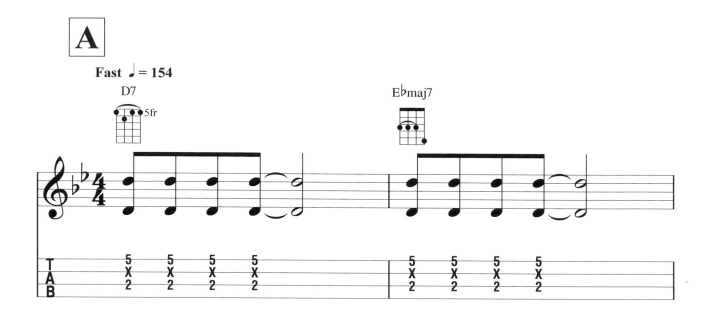

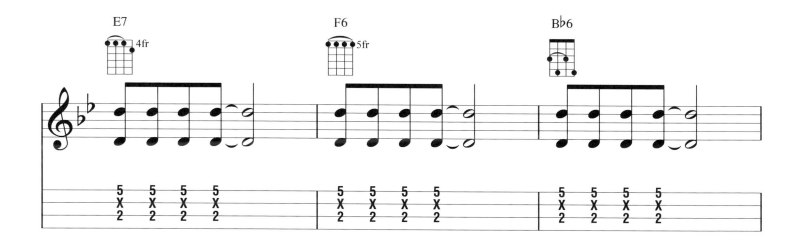

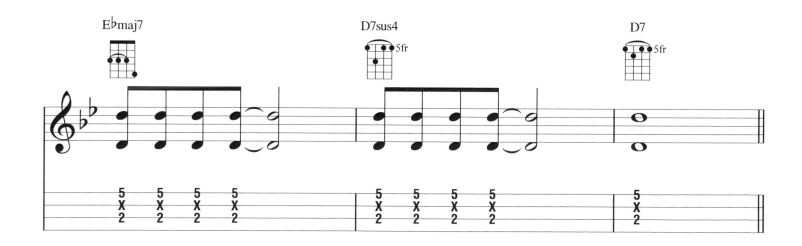

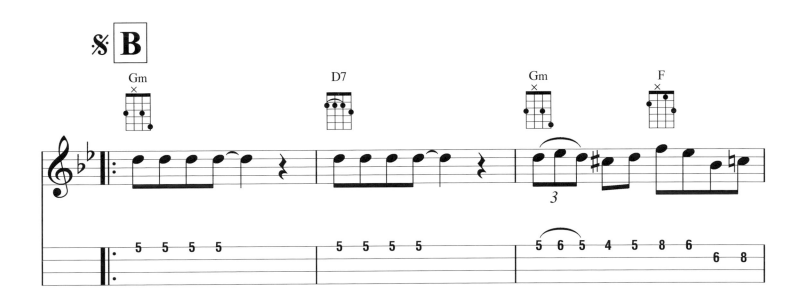

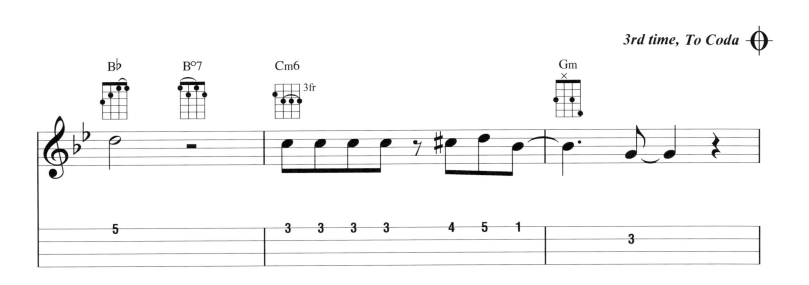

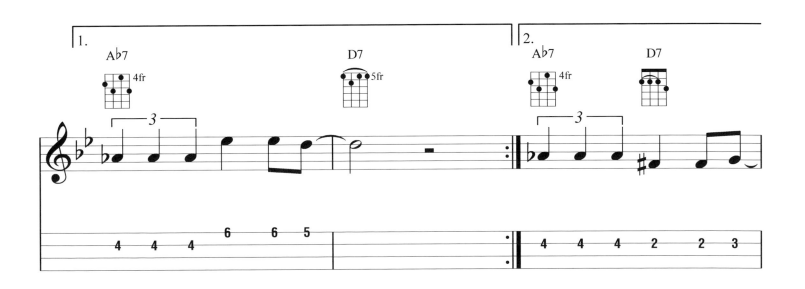

On Play Along track, form is played once through starting at A.
Then repeat back to B and play B B C B 2 times.

Minor Swing

By Django Reinhardt and Stephane Grappelli

*Ukulele 1 is removed on Play Along track.
**Chord symbols reflect implied harmony.

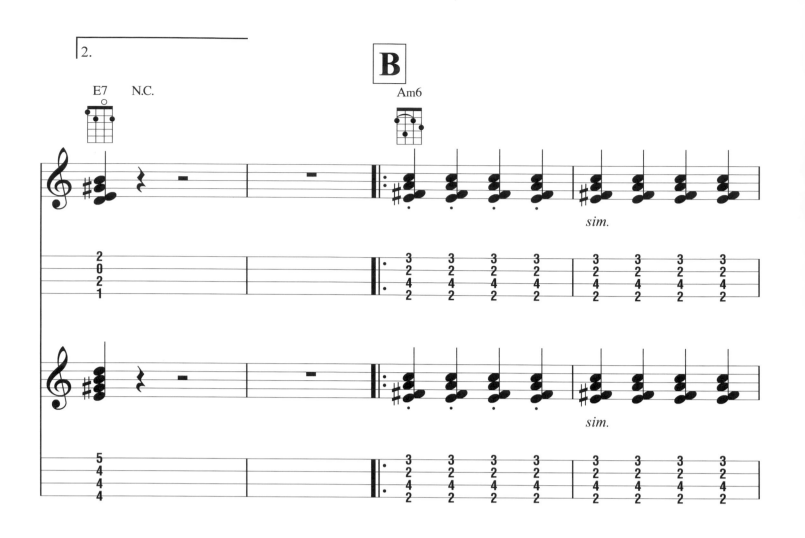

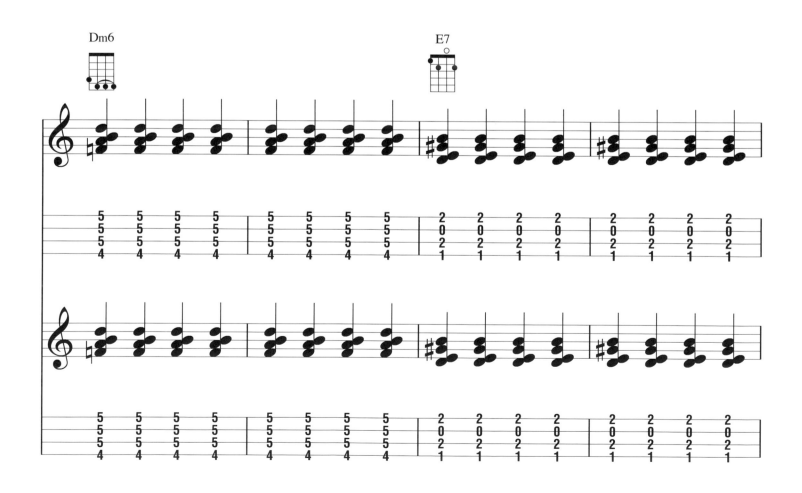

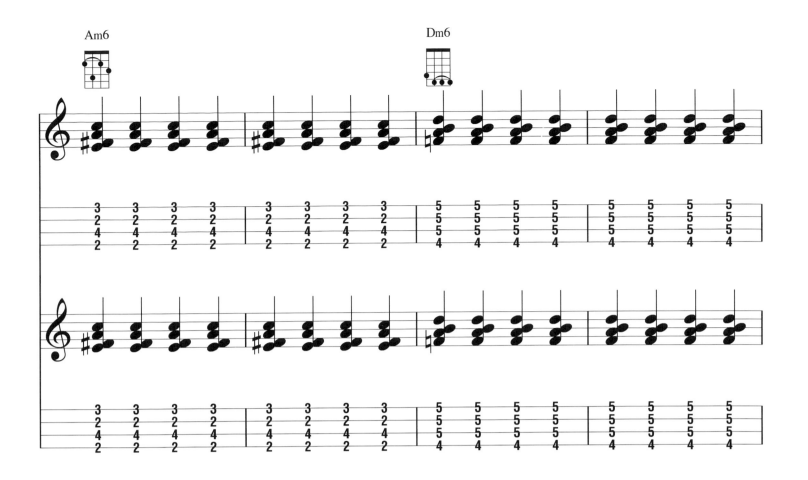

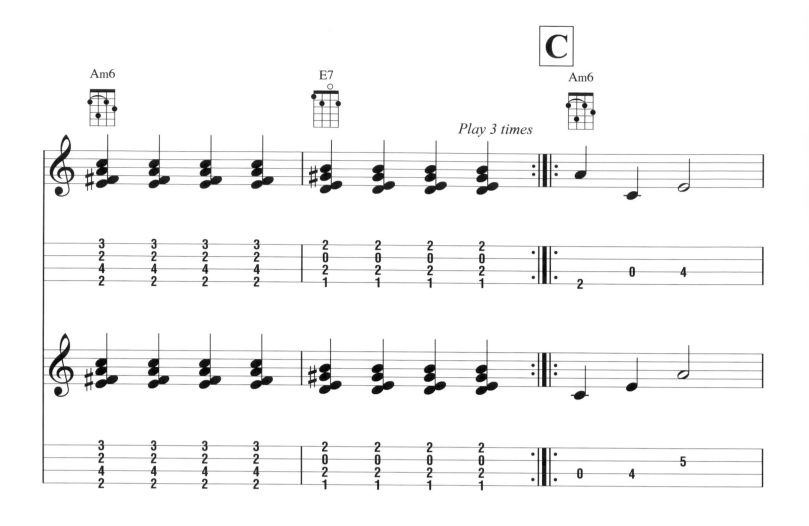

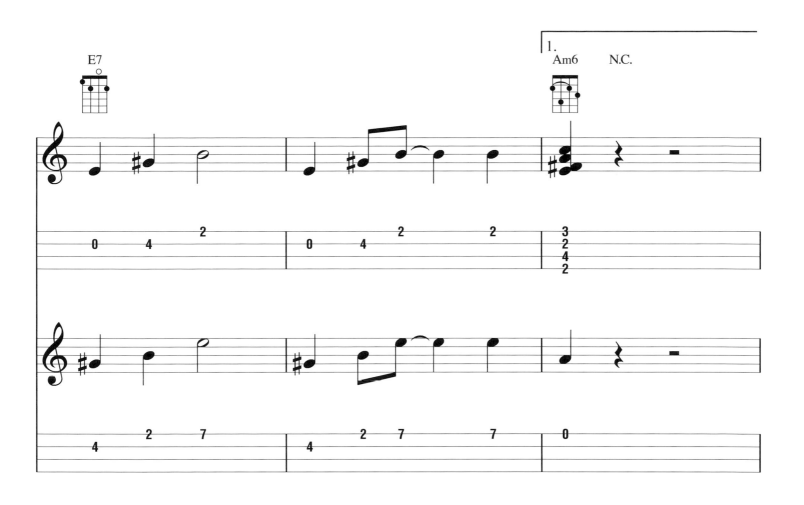

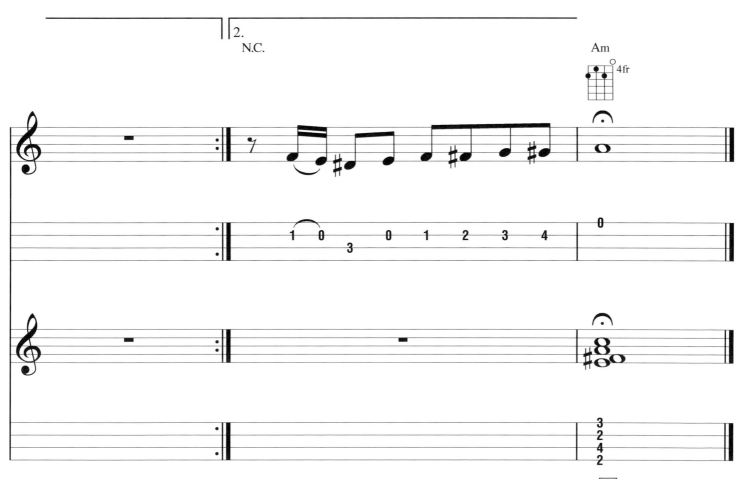

On Play Along track, B is played 5 times.

J'Attendrai

Words by Louis Poterat
Music by Dino Olivieri

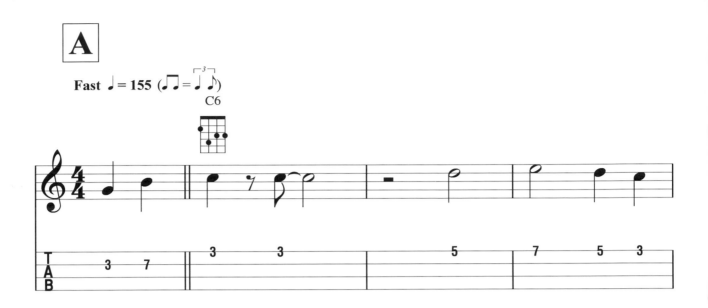

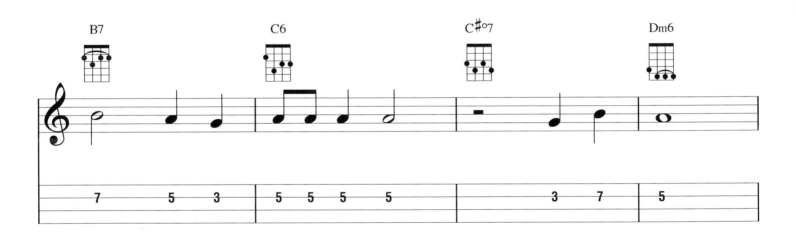

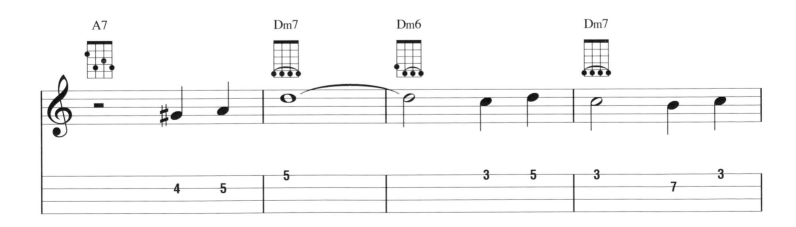

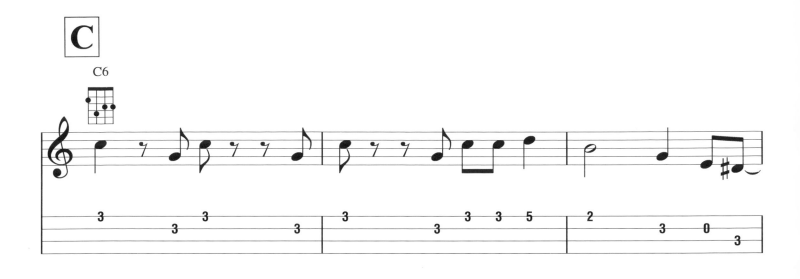

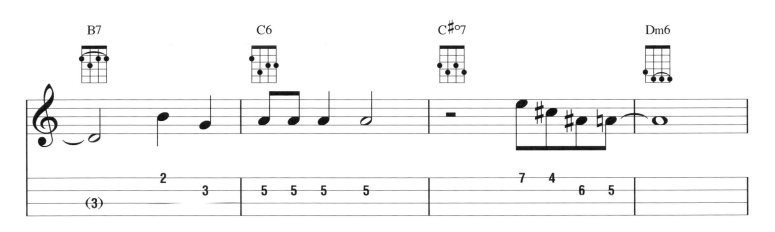

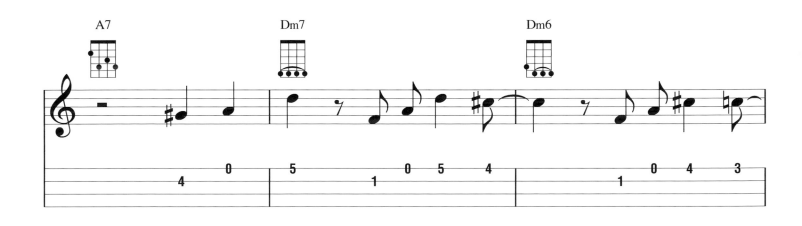

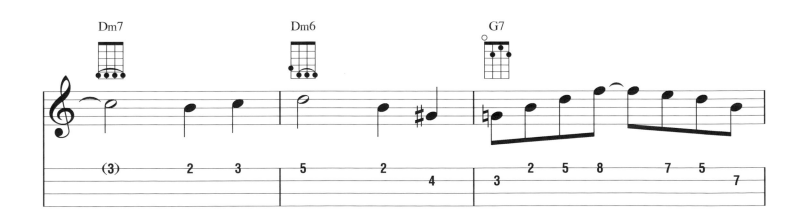

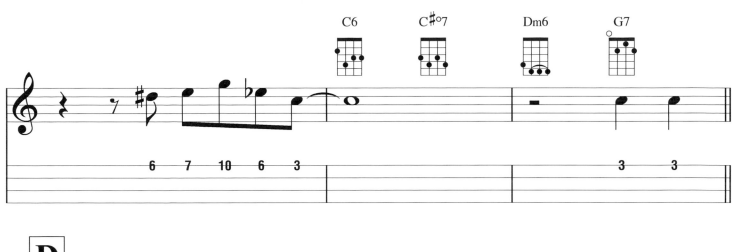

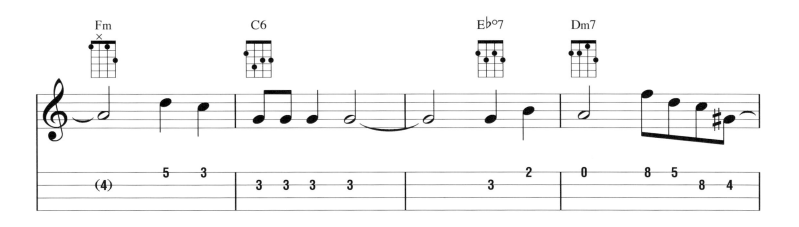

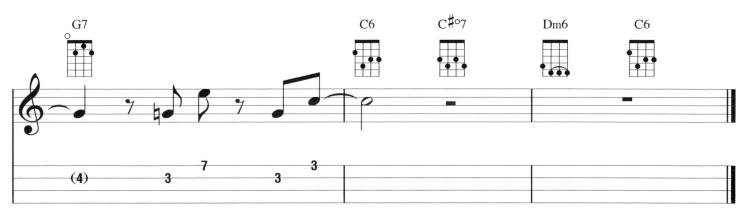

On Play Along track, form is played 2 times.

La Vie En Rose
(Take Me to Your Heart Again)

Original French Lyrics by Edith Piaf
Music by Luis Guglielmi
English Lyrics by Mack David

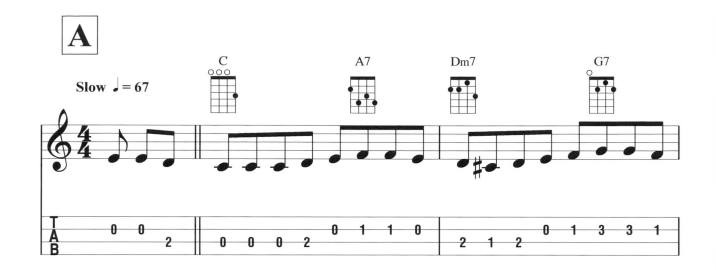

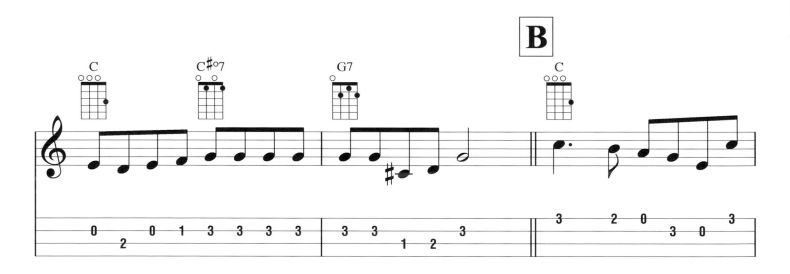

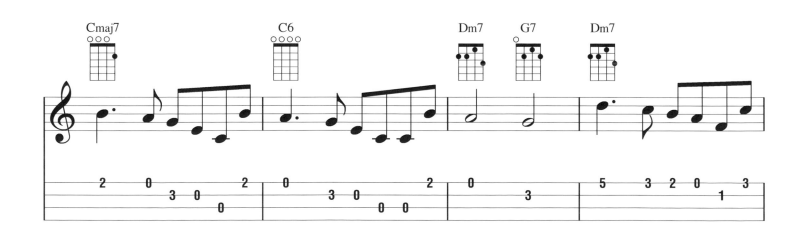

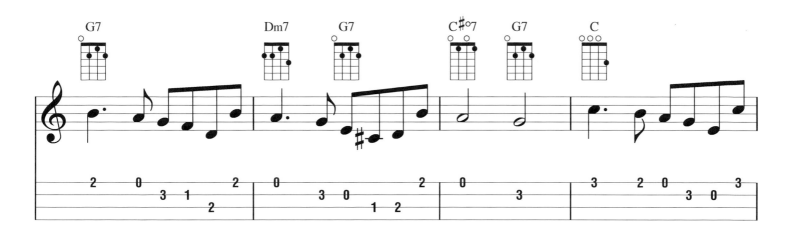

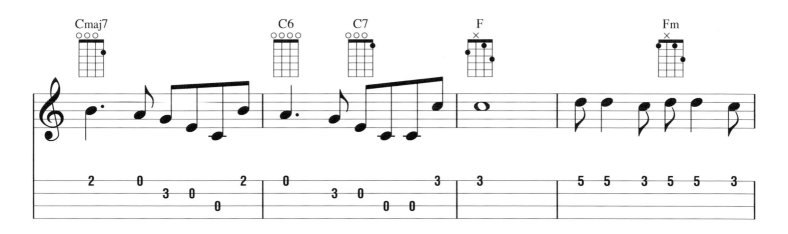

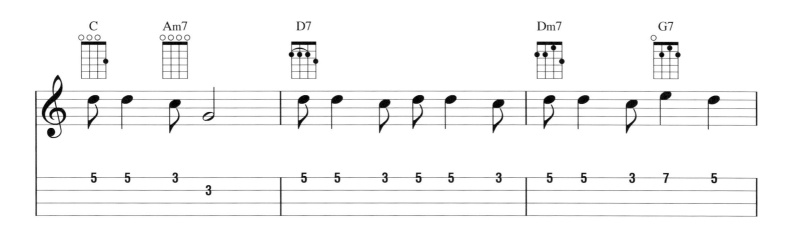

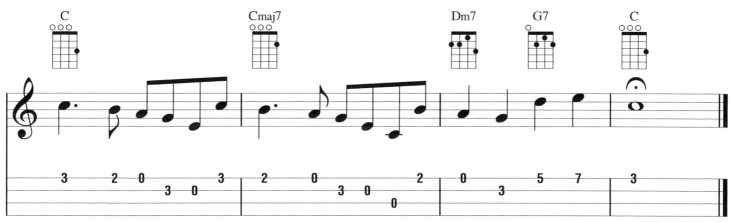

On Play Along track, form is played once starting at A .
Then repeat B 2 times.

Sweet Georgia Brown

Words and Music by Ben Bernie, Maceo Pinkard and Kenneth Casey

On Play Along track, form is played 4 times.

Nuages

By Django Reinhardt and Jacques Larue

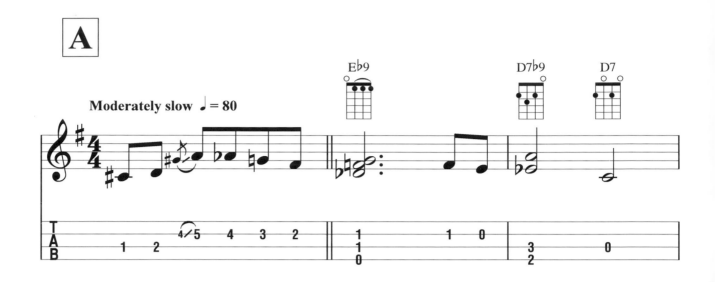

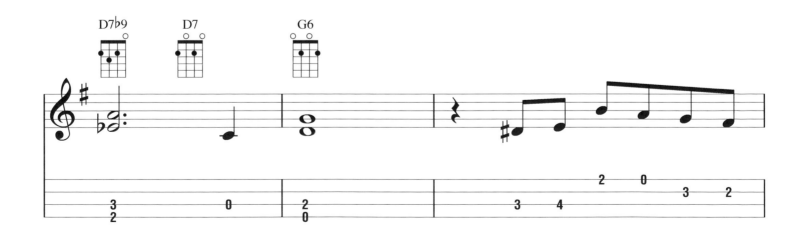

On Play Along track, form is played 2 times.